Whole Hearted

12 weeks of prayers to live fully while
waiting for something different

By Emily Culmer

Whole Hearted: 12 weeks of prayers to live fully while waiting for something different
Copyright © 2025 by Emily Culmer

ISBN: ISBN: 979-8-9936242-0-4

Unless otherwise noted, Scripture quotations are taken from the Holy Bible, New Living Translation (NLT), copyright ©1996, 2004, 2015 by Tyndale House Foundation. Used by permission of Tyndale House Publishers, Inc., Carol Stream, Illinois 60188. All rights reserved.

Printed in the United States of America
ISBN: [Insert if you have one or leave blank for now]
Contact: EmilyCulmer.com

Table of Contents

Week 1

Welcome to Whole Hearted. I'm so glad you're here.

Over the past year I have started praying for marriage. I went through a 100 days of intentional prayer and realized I had never thought much about what I want or need, let alone prayed about it. This journal is for all single women pursuing a Godly relationships, but it's especially for my chronically and happily single friends who late in their 20s/30s are realizing maybe we want something different.

In 2021, I was between jobs, in grad school, feeling like I was left behind, and like God wasn't hearing my prayers. My good friend Taylor said, "Emily, maybe God is making you wait in this season to prepare you for a longer or harder season of waiting and you need to grow your faith now." Spoiler alert, she was right. He heard my prayers and answered all of them with a "yes!" I'm not saying He's going to do that with my prayers about marriage, but I am saying He has a good track record of being faithful!

Every week for the next 12 weeks we're going to pray and journal with different focuses. Week one is all about praying when we don't feel like God is listening, and praying in faith hoping He'll answer but not being too confident.

We're going to reflect on how He answered us in the past, write short prayers we can pray anytime we doubt. Remembering God always answers even if we don't realize, or like the answer.

We're going to process why we haven't asked God for a husband before, and get real about our fears, struggles, and lies we believe about ourselves. But we're also going to dream, hope, and become more like Christ with a stronger faith to carry with us in every season of waiting.

Day 1

DDo you ever get so tired of praying the same prayer you begin to feel like maybe God's not actually listening to you? Like when you're on the phone and accidentally mute the call. I have felt that way in a few seasons of life; one of them being right now.

Here's what I want you to do: write down a very short version of what you have been praying over and over, your "elevator pitch" to God. Something you can pray over and over without it feeling long-winded. Then read Luke 18:1–8 then journal about it, tell God how it feels to keep praying and not seeing anything change.

_____

_____

_____

_____

_____

_____

_____

_____

_____

_____

_____

_____

_____

_____

Day 2

I don't know about you, but praying about finding the right person to date sometimes feels like sending a prayer to an empty abyss. You keep doing it because maybe God will answer. In seasons of waiting, it's easy to forget all the answered prayers we're living in today. My hardest seasons of waiting produced the strongest faith. Sometimes I let the lies that He won't answer override the history that He always answers, and His answers are always good!

Write out all the answered prayers you're living; everything you can think of. Thank God for answering those prayers and for how He answered them. Then, in faith that He will answer again, pray the short prayer you wrote yesterday.

_____

_____

_____

_____

_____

_____

_____

_____

_____

_____

_____

Day 3

Yesterday we thanked God for the answered prayers we're living in right now; then, in faith, asked God for the relationship we're longing for. For many of us, nothing changed overnight, it might still feel like we're praying and God's not moving. A few years ago, I was praying for a relationship, not because I wanted one, but because I was lonely. Instead of a guy, God gave me a youth group co-leader who, over the past three years, has become one of my closest friends. God answered the prayer so differently than I thought; He gave me what I needed and what I actually wanted. Here's what I want you to do: think back on every time you prayed for something specific and God answered in a wildly different way.

_____

_____

_____

_____

_____

_____

_____

_____

_____

_____

_____

_____

Day 4

Have you heard the phrase "God, if it's not your best for me, I don't want it." In a very low season of praying for the return of a relationship I thought had to be God's best, because it felt like the only option, I said, "What do you do when God's version of better is your version of what the hell?" What do we do? We pray. We ask God to reveal His best for us so clearly there's no way we could miss it. We ask God what work we need to do to be ready to say yes when he shows up. And we say in faith, "God, if he's not Your best, I'll wait for who is," then we release and obey.
Take some time to pray through these things, being bold in prayer and action.

_____

_____

_____

_____

_____

_____

_____

_____

_____

_____

_____

_____

Day 5

Do you hear people say, "If you stop looking you'll find someone," and want to lose your mind? If you're like me and have been perpetually single, I always want to say, "I was never looking, so it should have happened." I believe that's true for some, but for most people, they have to be looking to find their person. I spent a lot of years not looking, in part because I didn't believe someone was looking for me.

Write down every lie you have believed about why you're not in a relationship. Then read and journal through Psalm 139. Realizing I am deeply loved and known by the Creator of the universe helps me remember I am worth looking for, I am worth loving, and so are you.

_____

_____

_____

_____

_____

_____

_____

_____

_____

_____

_____

_____

Day 6

Jeremiah 29:12–13 "In those days when you pray, I will listen. If you look for me wholeheartedly, you will find me."

In Jeremiah, the people are being held in exile, mistreated in a land that is not their home. They are reminded of God's faithfulness to answer their calls. Being single isn't the same as being in exile, but in some Christian communities it's really isolating.

If you don't see God's people showing up for you in a hard season, pray for community to surround you, and challenge yourself to be real with one person about how you're feeling in this season.

Write about the hurt and hardships you're feeling right now about being single, then read those prayers out loud and ask God to comfort you in your season of waiting.

_____

_____

_____

_____

_____

_____

_____

_____

_____

_____

_____

Day 7

In my last hard season of waiting, a good friend asked me if I felt like God was using that season to prepare me for a longer, harder season of waiting. As much as I wished she was wrong, I knew the moment she asked that she was right. In that season of waiting I prayed less than I like to admit, but God answered all those prayers with yes, and they're all better than what I could have dreamed.

We're going to practice wild faith. I want you to pray tonight like God is going to answer all your marriage prayers with a "Yes, and!" What are you praying for? Take some time to write down the prayers of your wildest dreams.

_____

_____

_____

_____

_____

_____

_____

_____

_____

_____

_____

_____

Week Two

This week we're working through our past hurts. I know, feelings can be hard. I truly believe to be ready for the new, we have to process what was. For better or worse, the past is a part of our story, therefore part of who we are now and who we will be in relationships.

If we don't confront our past, we can't move into a healthy future. Have you been in a series of unhealthy situationships that impacted your value? We need to process why you allowed those, what you saw in those guys. In high school I honestly enjoyed friendships that felt more like dating than friendships. At that point in life, it came from a desire to live my own life and not wanting to deal with a boyfriend.

In college, when I continued to allow the same, it ended in feeling empty and like there was something about me that made me not worth committing to. Or there was something wrong with me; once they got too close, they went running the other way.

Some of us have to break lies and habits we believed because of the decisions we made or the ways guys treated us. Others have been told by our churches we need to be in a relationship and that it's more important than anything else. Some Christian communities confuse relationship status with spiritual maturity.

This week we are going to identify habits from past relationships you need to let go. We're going to take look at what the Bible says and stop believing lies about our singleness.

Day 1

There are multiple places throughout the Bible where singleness is praised. Paul writes about it as a gift that allows one to be focused on the things of God, having more capacity to serve. Being single, I have spent my 20's with an immense capacity to dedicate to discipleship. The amount of time I spend developing the next generation of Christian leaders would not be sustainable if I was also trying to sustain a serious relationship. We all have only so much to go around, and so many hours in the day. I am able to spend many of my hours talking for hours with students, leading groups, and pouring into my own relationship with God. It's a choice to see this season as a gift, and it's a choice to use it to honor God.

What are you doing with your gift of singleness? Are you using your time and capacity to honor and serve God?

_____

_____

_____

_____

_____

_____

_____

_____

_____

Day 2

Let's take stock of our past dating decisions. Are there wounds you need to heal? At some point maybe you allowed yourself to be treated as less than a woman deeply loved by God and created in God's image (Genesis 1).
Marriage is to be an earthly reflection of how Christ loved the church. Were you treated as though you had that value? If yes, how did it feel? If no, why?
Ask God to heal any wounds and give you the strength to wait for a man who reflects His character and treats you as precious.

_____
_____
_____
_____
_____
_____
_____
_____
_____
_____
_____
_____
_____

Day 3

Yesterday we asked for healing for wounds from past relationships. Today we need to own our role in those wounds. I know for me, there was a core belief allowing those decisions. I believed what I had was the best I would ever have, and it was better than nothing. But what I learned: it's not. Being single is better than being unhappy; being with no one is better than being with the wrong one.

What are the core lies that led you to allow the past relationships? Ask God to reveal His truth into those lies.

_____

_____

_____

_____

_____

_____

_____

_____

_____

_____

_____

_____

_____

Day 4

Continuing to look back, what was good about your past experiences or guys you liked? What were the values and character traits you were attracted to? What elements of your past relationships were good, and helped you grow in your faith? Identifying the good will help you know what to look for going forward.
Ask God to reveal what they had along with what you need.

_____

_____

_____

_____

_____

_____

_____

_____

_____

_____

_____

_____

_____

_____

_____

Day 5

We all have pain points that affect the relationships we have today. Not just in dating, but also in our friendships, workplaces, and the ways we build and maintain trust. Because of my upbringing I struggle with believing I would be anyone's first choice. That's a scar I carry and have to be aware of in all my relationships.
What are your pain points? What do you need to do today to start healing?
Ask God to reveal your pain points and how you can begin healing so you're ready to love and be loved.

_____

_____

_____

_____

_____

_____

_____

_____

_____

_____

_____

_____

_____

_____

Day 6

Marriage isn't a prerequisite to be a leader in the church. I know that may be a really jarring sentence to read, if it is, i want you to pause and let it sink in. Have you started believing your singleness is tied to your spirituality? As soon as you start doing X or stop doing Y, then maybe God will let you have a relationship? I genuinely do not believe God that's how works.

Confess what you have believed about your spirituality and singleness. Then ask God to make the truth of how He works real to you to right this belief.

_____

_____

_____

_____

_____

_____

_____

_____

_____

_____

_____

_____

_____

Day 7

A lie I had to combat was that my adult life didn't start until I was married. For generations of women this was a reality, but it's not anymore. You can begin living a full and meaningful life before you're married. Living a full life will likely help you meet your future husband. Research shows the younger a woman is when she gets married, the more likely the marriage will end in divorce. Often, women feel trapped or discontent with married life because they didn't get to do certain things before getting married and having a family.

What are some things you want to do before you get married? What are things you feel like you can't do until you're married? Pray about what it would look like to start doing those things and living the fullest life you can now.

_____

_____

_____

_____

_____

_____

_____

_____

_____

_____

_____

Week 3

For a long time, I believed being perpetually single meant something was wrong with me; or I wasn't a good candidate for a relationship. I compared myself to every girl who was dating, thinking if I became more like her, maybe I'd have a chance. Other times, I'd focus only on the flaws I saw in other relationships, using that as a false sense of comfort for staying single.

Eventually, all that energy turned inward, and I fixated on everything I thought was "wrong" with me. I used to say, "I'm confident in every area of my life...except dating." I lost sight of the truth: I was intentionally created by a powerful God. I was so focused on the one relationship I didn't have I overlooked my flourishing, and life-giving relationships.

This week, we're shifting our focus. Instead of dwelling on what we don't have, we'll celebrate what we do. We'll reflect on our God-given identity and value discovering how those truths shape the way we show up in every relationship.

Here are some big-picture questions to guide us: Which relationships in your life are healthy? How do they make you feel? In what ways do they help you become the best version of yourself? Who is that best version of you?

Day 1

In the past, when I have prayed for a relationship, I was pleading a case with God on why someone would be a good match for me; or how I could shape-shift myself into being a good match for him. We want to be with someone who reflects Christ back to us and helps us grow, while also loving and accepting us exactly as we are.

Think through your relationships your life and why you're a good friend, sister, daughter, aunt, etc. Which of those traits will help you be a good wife and maybe one day a good mom?

Then pray asking God to help you see a fuller picture of who He created you to be. So when you meet the right man, you're confident enough to fully be yourself.

_____

_____

_____

_____

_____

_____

_____

_____

_____

_____

_____

_____

Day 2

At some point, most of us have believed a lie about who we need to become in order to be in a relationship. Maybe you've been told you're "too much" or "a lot to handle." Maybe you've felt pressure to be more: put yourself out there, flirt more, change to fit into someone else's mold.

The truth is this: we're meant to show up exactly as God created us. The right person needs to know and love the real you. Your one precious life shouldn't be spent shrinking your gifts just to make someone else more comfortable.

Write everything you bring to a relationship. What qualities make you a great friend? Are you loyal, empathetic, generous, thoughtful? List every strength and characteristic you can think of, and thank God for the way He's uniquely designed you.

_____

_____

_____

_____

_____

_____

_____

_____

_____

_____

_____

Day 3

Whether or not you have been in romantic relationships, you have relationships; hopefully some of them are healthy. I want you to take some time to think about your best relationships, the ones that leave you feeling refreshed and most like yourself. What do they all have in common? What traits do the other people in those relationships have? How can you be looking for those same traits in a husband?

_____

_____

_____

_____

_____

_____

_____

_____

_____

_____

_____

_____

_____

_____

_____

_____

Day 4

At some point most of us have told being single is a failure. We have been told our standards are too high. We failed to put ourselves out there enough. We said no to an okay or even good guy and therefore ruined our chances.

Now there may be some truth to these statements. You may have said no to someone great because you weren't ready. Maybe you spend all your time at home hoping Amazon delivers a perfect guy within 48 hours.

Take some time to pray through the things you've been told. Ask God to show you which of those are lies you've started to believe as truth; then consider what is actually true and where He might be inviting you to grow.

_____
_____
_____
_____
_____
_____
_____
_____
_____
_____
_____
_____

Day 5

Last week we unpacked wounds we need to let scar so we can have healthier relationships. At times I believed my scars somehow made me broken or unlovable. The root of that belief was thinking God was not big enough to heal my wounds, or good enough to create someone who would love me anyway. I believed something God had handcrafted (me) wasn't good enough to be loved. This way of thinking is sinful and doesn't recognize the all-powerful nature of God.

What beliefs about yourself deny the all-powerful ways of God? Confess them here, and if you're brave enough, with a trusted friend or mentor so they can speak life into your brokenness.

_____

_____

_____

_____

_____

_____

_____

_____

_____

_____

_____

_____

_____

_____

Day 6

I believe there is so much power in saying things out loud. Throughout scripture we always see prayer as spoken aloud.

I want you to read the following passages and write I am statements- I am God's masterpiece. When you're done I want you to stand in the mirror and read them out loud. Genesis 1:27, Psalm 139, John 1:12, 2 Corinthians 5:17, 1 Peter 2:9, Ephesians 2:10, Romans 8:15–16, Romans 8:38–39, Philippians 3:20

Day 7

Ephesians 2:10 says we are God's masterpiece. Words associated with masterpiece are: priceless, perfect, without fault, desired, sought out, captivating. Seeing ourselves as anything less is to downplay God's masterpiece. Genesis 1:27, God gives people the stamp of "very good" or perfect. When I look at myself compared to the ocean, I feel like I pale in comparison. But not to God. Matthew 6:26 says we're the most valuable creation.

Do you believe this? Do you live like this? Treat other people like this? Date like this? Pray through these questions and ask God to make clear the truth of your identity.

_____
_____
_____
_____
_____
_____
_____
_____
_____
_____
_____
_____
_____

Week 4

Let's talk about friendship. I think the some of the most important relationships in our lives are our friendships. Friends help shape us into who we are; they teach us how to be close to people we're not related to and how to connect and grow.

It's scientifically proven that we become the average of the five people we spend the most time with. Like it or not, you become like your friends. My pastor always says, "Show me your friends, and I'll show you your future." He means this in terms of what they're pursuing and who you will become. I also mean it in how they treat you and what you learn to expect from a dating relationship.

The truth is, if we put up with not being a priority in friendships, we're not going to expect anything different in dating or marriage. The friends I've had throughout my 20s and now 30s have raised the bar for what I expect in a husband.

My friends, specifically my best friend, have shown up for me in every season of life. When I have been thriving, happy, and confident, she's there. When I have been in the hardest seasons of my life, she is there. She shows up when she's asked to and, more importantly, when she's needed but not asked. She knows me deeply and has been my safe place throughout almost a decade of life.

Most of my friends have kids, and even more are married. In most circles, I am the lone single person. They never for a second make me feel othered, less valued, less welcomed, or like a burden. They also don't treat me as a glorified nanny; I'm simply another person in the group.

I am celebrated and loved just as I am. This is true friendship, and what I hope you can have or find. We're going to talk about the influence of our friends, thank God for the good ones, and become better ones ourselves. Friendship is great relational training ground and where you start to decide what you do and do not want in a future marriage.

Day 1

I have amazing friends now, but that wasn't always the case.

Take some time to reflect on the following: Do you share your faith and mutually support each other? Are your friendships free of competition? If you're becoming the average of your friends, are they leading you toward heaven or toward harm?

If these answers are positive, thank God for your friends; for how they reflect Him and help you become more Christlike. If not, pray and ask God to surround you with deep and meaningful friendships.

_____

_____

_____

_____

_____

_____

_____

_____

_____

_____

_____

_____

Day 2

Some of the earliest written records of female friendship come from the Bible. We often hear about the great love of Ruth and Boaz, but before Ruth and Boaz, there was Ruth and Naomi. You should read their whole story, it's only about five pages. Naomi is the one who told Ruth about Boaz and helped her get near him. If not for Naomi, there would be no Ruth and Boaz. These women were deeply connected and loyal to one another before and after Boaz.

Are your friendships helping you become who you need to be when you meet your Boaz? Are they pushing toward a Godly man? Are they helping you become a Godly woman who would attract a Godly man?

_____

_____

_____

_____

_____

_____

_____

_____

_____

_____

_____

Day 3

Finding a significant other isn't going to make you less lonely. Healing your loneliness comes from rich community, and I would go as far to say faith based community. What does community look life for you right now? Is it want for yourself now, and even into the future?

Pray about your community, that God would sustain it, or maybe provide it. Ask him to begin to heal the loneliness you feel in this season.

_____

_____

_____

_____

_____

_____

_____

_____

_____

_____

_____

_____

_____

_____

_____

Day 4

Over the years my best friend and I would say to each other, "If I ever do _____, remind me of this moment." We were talking about different ways women in our lives, or on our TVs, would lose their sense of identity in a relationship. We'd see them compromising their value to stay with someone rather than finding someone who loved all of them.

Are your friends honest with you? Would they tell you if you were drifting, settling, or with the wrong person? Are they willing to ask you hard questions and do you care enough to listen? Have you given them permission to speak into the most precious parts of your life?

_____

_____

_____

_____

_____

_____

_____

_____

_____

_____

_____

Day 5

Yesterday we talked about friends who value you. Today I want to flip that question: do you value your friends?

The reason Naomi was able to help Ruth find Boaz is because Ruth trusted her enough to listen and follow her encouragement. Do you trust your friends' input on faith, finances, life decisions, and dating? If they're not pointing you toward God, they're pushing you away from Him.

Pray for friends who continually point you back to God and for the humility to listen when they give wise advice.

Day 6

Proverbs 17:17 says a friend loves at all times, a brother is there in adversity.
Ruth and Naomi cemented their friendship in a time of deep adversity, and developed a familial relationship. Unlike your family, you get to choose all your friends. The only member of your family you'll choose is your husband.
Reflect on your friendships, how have you chosen? Are they there in a time of adversity? Have you cemented your friendship in fire, or have a sisterhood born from bonding together in adversity?

_____

_____

_____

_____

_____

_____

_____

_____

_____

_____

_____

_____

_____

_____

Day 7

Earlier I mentioned that my best friend has shown up for me in my best and worst seasons, when I asked, and when I didn't. Because of that, she has raised the bar for how I expect to be treated in a relationship.

Are you allowing people to love you, show up for you, celebrate you, and speak into your life? Are you doing the same for them? How have your friends reflected Christ to you? In what ways are they helping set your relational standards?

_____

_____

_____

_____

_____

_____

_____

_____

_____

_____

_____

_____

_____

_____

_____

Week 5

What was the first moment you realized you wanted something different? I can pinpoint mine to the minute. I was leaving Easter brunch with my friends and was the only one getting in the car alone. One couple had two kids, one had a baby, and the other had just told us they were expecting their first. We started off all single, and to see everyone really grow up together and become married with kids was beautiful. Typically, I left those events feeling so full, grateful for my community but content with going home to a quiet house. As I got in my car, and drove away, I felt really alone. The stillness and quiet of the car, and house felt so loud. It was no longer what I wanted.

We all have a moment of realizing something we have is no longer what we want. It could be a job, car, haircut, roommate—anything. At some point, what we have stops serving us, runs its course, and pushes us to make a change.

For me, it was the lonely drive home and the realization I wanted something different. I wanted someone to share my quiet moments, someone to be there when everyone goes home. It's not that my life suddenly felt meaningless, or I suddenly felt like I wasn't enough. It's that what had served me for the past 30 years wasn't going to serve me for the next 30 years.

Though I had dated and had a few situtationships, I hadn't wanted something permanent or long-term. I hadn't wanted a husband; I hadn't moved from seeing a guy as good company and a means to doubling my income. I had put no thought into what I wanted or who I was looking for. I had a friend ask what I was looking for, and I said, "30ish and emotionally available." They laughed before realizing I wasn't joking. I wasn't joking because I had literally no idea what I was looking for, and wouldn't have known it if he walked right in front of me.

This week is for thinking and praying through what you're looking for. What do you want in life and marriage? What do you want him to be like? If he walked right in front of you, would you know what you're looking for enough to realize it was him?

Day 1

Something happened to get you here, not just here in this journal but her to ordering this book, then to making it to week 5. What was it? What was the moment you felt like what you had no longer fit?

Pray about everything you felt in the moment, then how you feel now. Do you still want it as bad? More? Are you afraid or hopeful? Bring God into all those feelings.

_____

_____

_____

_____

_____

_____

_____

_____

_____

_____

_____

_____

_____

_____

_____

_____

Day 2

Today I want you do to a word dump, just get out everything you think of when you think of marraige and your future husband. Good, bad the messy.
Put it on paper and give it all to God.

_____

_____

_____

_____

_____

_____

_____

_____

_____

_____

_____

_____

_____

_____

_____

_____

_____

_____

_____

Day 3

For years, what kept me from wanting a relationship was a deeply held belief it would demand that I give up or change everything in my life. Now, I no longer believe that to be true; however, it would likely require some things to change. Prayerfully consider things in your life you would be willing to change for the sake of a relationship. Are you willing to change churches, find a different job, see your friends or family less.

Write them all out and ask God to guide you in what you need to surrender.

_____

_____

_____

_____

_____

_____

_____

_____

_____

_____

_____

_____

_____

_____

Day 4

Yesterday we prayed about things in our life that could change to make space for a relationship. Today we're going to think about the other side of that. Are there goals that you want to accomplish single or before you change your lifestyle? I wanted to live alone; that was something I valued and wouldn't have bent on. Now that I have for years, I'm okay with it changing. What about your life are you not willing to change? Could be family obligations, church, etc., but what holds such deep value it's a not negotiable for you?

Be prayerful, try to make this list short and focused on what you value really deeply. Be bold and maybe go back to the pages from yesterday and offer a few more things for change.

_____

_____

_____

_____

_____

_____

_____

_____

_____

_____

_____

Day 5

I mentioned when I realized I wanted something different, I had no idea what I wanted in a husband. I want you to make a list of character traits you're hoping for in your future husband. Not in the 6'5, blue eyes way, but in the: kind, empathetic, feels things because I don't kind of way.
Ask God to reveal what you need in a partner be balanced? Name them here, and pray to see them when they walk by.

_____

_____

_____

_____

_____

_____

_____

_____

_____

_____

_____

_____

_____

_____

Day 6

Have you thought about what you want the rest of your life to look like? Again, I'm talking big picture and values. The truth is there are probably a lot of men you would be compatible with who have the character you're looking for, but they have to be going where you're going. Do you want kids, want to work, to travel, to move abroad or live on a farm? You need to be with someone who sees those same things for their life. You need to fit as you were created, not as you have shape-shifted yourself to match with someone else.

Pray and ask God to give you vision for the life He has for you, and to see where a husband and maybe a family would fit into that.

_____

_____

_____

_____

_____

_____

_____

_____

_____

_____

_____

_____

_____

_____

Day 7

Now that you have some vision for what you want in life and in a husband, I want you to pray for the following things:

Ability to see him when he comes into your life.

Patience to trust God's timing and not force anything.

For him as he waits for you.

_____
_____
_____
_____
_____
_____
_____
_____
_____
_____
_____
_____
_____
_____
_____
_____

Week 6

What are your values and priorities? I'm talking in the faith, parenthood, how you spend your money way. You need to know your values, what values you feel like you would be willing to bend or compromise on and what things are set in stone. Not in a "you have to change him" sense, but in a "you need to be naturally aligned" sense. You're not going to align everywhere, but somewhere you need to align.

In college, I briefly dated a guy and almost every time we were together I would leave feeling like something that felt important to me was either dismissed or not important to him. He was not my match.

With a different guy I liked but didn't date, I always felt like I had to hide parts of myself. I felt like if he saw the whole, or unrefined parts of me that were different from him, I would have no chance of being with him.

The truth with both was that God was protecting me from being with guys who were not my match. He had someone better in mind for all of us.

This week we're going to process who we are at our core. We're going to pray about who we are becoming and what kind of life God has in store. We're going to process what we won't bend on and areas where we're open to evolving. It's going to be hard work, but I promise you this: it's way better to be single and living a life we love than to be married and dreaming of the life we could have had if we had held out for God's best.

We were created with so much intention and purpose. If God is powerful enough to create you with so much value, then He is powerful enough to create someone who loves and chooses you in all your forms, and was created to partner with you in life.

Day 1

Before you can know what values you won't compromise you need to revist what you bring to the table. I know we did this a few weeks ago, but hopefully in the past month how you see yourself has evolved.

What do you bring to a relationships? How do you show others love? What is your greatest strgenth in a relationship? What about you easy to love? How do you reflect God's character?

_____
_____
_____
_____
_____
_____
_____
_____
_____
_____
_____
_____
_____
_____

Day 2

Yesterday you reflected on your relational gifting. Today, take some time to think about your values; the core principles that shape who you are and how you live. In healthy relationships, one person's strengths often complement the other's weaknesses. For some, that means valuing decisiveness; for others, it might mean emotional depth or compassion.

Think about where you are weak and what values you need your future partner to share or strengthen in you. Pray for clarity and honesty as you identify what truly matters to you and what you need in a godly relationship.

_____

_____

_____

_____

_____

_____

_____

_____

_____

_____

_____

_____

_____

_____

Day 3

One of my core values is serving in the church, and recently I've felt convicted about wanting a husband who shares that same heart for service. A friend of mine shared that one of her values is hospitality and having an open home.
What's something you're doing now that you hope to continue with your future husband? Take time to pray for clarity and vision about what God has for your future.

_____

_____

_____

_____

_____

_____

_____

_____

_____

_____

_____

_____

_____

_____

_____

Day 4

As we spend a week praying about service and partnership, I want you to list out all the ways you serve in the church and who you're leading.

Pray about what it would look like to do that while married. Do you want your partner by your side? Are you okay serving in very different ways? How would he encourage the ways you're serving?

_____

_____

_____

_____

_____

_____

_____

_____

_____

_____

_____

_____

_____

_____

Day 5

As a single woman, hopefully you manage your own finances. What are your financial priorities? How do you feel about debt, do you have any, and would you be okay marrying into debt? Do you tithe? Do you tend to spend on things or on experiences? How do you feel about credit cards?

Take some time to pray about your financial priorities. Then, decide what you would be willing to adjust in marriage.

_____

_____

_____

_____

_____

_____

_____

_____

_____

_____

_____

_____

_____

_____

_____

_____

Day 6

I think something assumed a lot in Christian communities is everyone wants kids, but it's not the case. You need to spend some time thinking and praying about if you want kids. Are you open but okay either way? Super opposed or eagerly awaiting being a mom? Do you want to adopt or foster? Are you able to biologically have kids or are there medical conditions that will prevent you from having kids? Anywhere you land on the spectrum is okay, but you need to be real about where you land.

Pray about all these things and ask God to make your desires very clear. Then ask for boldness to articulate them to a potential husband when the time comes.

_____

_____

_____

_____

_____

_____

_____

_____

_____

_____

_____

_____

Day 7

As you think about values, it's important to think about boundaries. What are relational, emotional and physical boundaries you want to keep? There is no guarantee the next guy you date is going to be your husband.
What do you feel comfortable telling him and when? What do you feel comfortable doing with him? Pray for clarity on your feeling toward this, and ability to set and mantain boundaries that refelct your convitcion.

_____

_____

_____

_____

_____

_____

_____

_____

_____

_____

_____

_____

_____

_____

Week 7

How do you love others, and how do you want to be loved?

How do you reflect God's character? What areas are you naturally weaker in and want to grow? How do you need a partner to help make you more Christlike?

Do you have any specific convictions about ways you want to serve with your future husband? Are there things you deeply value and want to be sure he values as well — things like serving, an open-door policy at home, tithing, etc.?

How are you serving at church or helping others grow? What would it look like to do that with a husband?

What are your financial priorities, and which of those would you be open to changing? How can the women in this group help you learn to be more financially literate?

Share your feelings around kids with your group. Do you want them or not? So far as you know, are you able to have them? Would you be willing to marry someone who already has them? Process these big questions together.

What are your emotional and spiritual boundaries? How have you and other women let those progress in relationships? If you have done this well or poorly, share your experience. If this is new for you, listen, take note, and ask good questions as you process your boundaries.

Day 1

Before you dive into a week of thinking about your physical boundaries, take some time to decide what it really means for you to save yourself for marriage. The Bible is very clear that sex was created for marriage, and only for marriage. What it doesn't do is spell out the exact line of "how far is too far." Here's the truth: if you're focused on finding the line, you're already asking the wrong question. We're not called to see how close we can get to sin, we're called to flee from sexual immorality (1 Corinthians 6:8).

In light of that, where do you notice yourself shifting from pursuing holiness to pursuing your own pleasure?

_____

_____

_____

_____

_____

_____

_____

_____

_____

_____

_____

_____

_____

_____

Day 2

Did you know that our brains create sexual neural pathways? They are triggered when our brain learns that an input (touch, thought, or media) leads to a reward or dopamine release. The more an input leads to a reward, the more reactive you become. When it comes to sexual boundaries, you need to set them for yourself before you introduce a potential partner to the situation. What you watch, read, and do contributes to you breaking your own boundaries.

Spend some time in prayer; ask God to help you take inventory of your input and feel convicted about what you need to remove.

_____
_____
_____
_____
_____
_____
_____
_____
_____
_____
_____
_____
_____

Day 3

Is the media you're consuming helping you protect your boundaries or pushing them? There is a lot of research on how porn impacts your brain sexually, and one could assume romance books have a similar effect.

How is what you consume inpacting your pursuit of holiness? What's okay and what do you feel convicted to remove? Pray for conviction, for the ability to pursue holiness rather than trying to justify how far is actually too far.

_____

_____

_____

_____

_____

_____

_____

_____

_____

_____

_____

_____

_____

_____

_____

Day 4

Before you can say I'm not going any further than _____ you need to decide the furthest you're willing to go. You have to work it backward. If you're not having sex, to not have sex can you do other things? Are you or are you not removing clothing? If you're not removing clothes what are you touching? Are you lying down, straddling, sitting up? Work it back words of if not this, the not x,y,z.
Be prayerful be specific and let your convictions lead you.

_____
_____
_____
_____
_____
_____
_____
_____
_____
_____
_____
_____
_____
_____
_____

Day 5

As Christians we talk a lot about sexual purity and not having sex. We pretty much never talk about what to do with our hormones and urges before marriage. Take some time to pray and journal about your feelings toward porn, romance books, masturbation. Remember, your brain creates pleasure pathways and those pathways are hard to unlearn.

Are the things you're doing helping you hold your boundaries or helping you push them? Where do you feel convicted to draw or redraw your boundaries?

_____
_____
_____
_____
_____
_____
_____
_____
_____
_____
_____
_____
_____
_____

Day 6

Something that made this feel real and important to me was learning how the habits I have now can impact my sex life with my future husband. Waiting over 30 years for marriage, only to struggle to fully enjoy it because I've trained my body to respond more to my own touch than my husband's, is not what I want for my future. If I'm waiting that long, I want to be able to enjoy it.

How are your habits now impacting your future sex life? Are you okay with them? Do you need to make changes now to protect that future? Pray for conviction and make an action plan.

_____

_____

_____

_____

_____

_____

_____

_____

_____

_____

_____

_____

_____

Day 7

In praying for my future marriage, I wrote the prayer, "Let him choose protection over pleasure." What I meant in those words is: give him the strength to choose to protect sex within our marriage one day, instead of giving himself pleasure now.
What big prayer do you want to pray for yourself and your future husband to protect your future sex lives?

_____

_____

_____

_____

_____

_____

_____

_____

_____

_____

_____

_____

_____

_____

_____

Week 8

This week we're going to pray about God's plans for our lives and who we need to have by our sides to see those plans come true.

I have heard the words, "It would take someone special to handle all of you." They were spoken as a joke and by someone who loves me, but they didn't feel like a joke, and a decade later they still ring in my mind. They caused me to believe not only am I too difficult to love, but someone wouldn't want to sign up to be a part of what I'm doing. They feed the lie of being too much, too intimidating to men, and breaking the mold of what a Christian woman 'should' be.

The reality is, the Bible is full of really powerful women, and some of them were likely very intimidating and strong. The Proverbs 31 woman was not a passive trad wife who spent all day barefoot and pregnant in the kitchen waiting for her husband to come home. She's a hard-working businesswoman providing for herself and her family, making big financial decisions; she is strong and kind and wise.

Priscilla is mentioned in multiple New Testament books as working and traveling with Paul. She was married to Aquila, but her name is ALWAYS listed first, showing her importance, value, and she likely held the primary role of teaching and leading the early church alongside Aquila.

As we spend the week praying through ministry and serving, we need to remember God equally values women, married and single, in service of the church. What does service look like now? How do you want that to evolve, and how does a partner factor in? Is your husband a partner in ministry and life? Do you desire to serve shoulder to shoulder? Those are the questions of the week, let's jump in.

Day 1

I want you to take some time to read and reread Proverbs 31. This is what a mother told her son to look for in the ideal wife.

What is she doing? How is she caring for her family and husband? What is she like? Are you like her? If so, how? If not, What steps can you take to become more like her? Do you know a woman like her? What do you think of her and how she loves and leads her family?

_____

_____

_____

_____

_____

_____

_____

_____

_____

_____

_____

_____

_____

Day 2

Spend a few minutes doing a quick search about Priscilla.

We can go out on a limb and say she was probably told at least once she was too much. Maybe she was told she was too loud or talked too much. She was probably told she wouldn't find someone who would travel with her while she told everyone about Jesus. We see in Scripture, she did. She found a strong partner in Aquila; he was likely so strong in his faith that he let her be strong in hers, and partnered his service with hers. He let her lean into her strength and stood by her side.

How does their marriage and ministry reflect what you desire for your own life? In light of that, what are some characteristics of the kind of man you're looking for?

_____

_____

_____

_____

_____

_____

_____

_____

_____

_____

_____

Day 3

I want you to take a few minutes to do a quick search about Phoebe.
Like Priscilla, she was a leader in the early church and likely was told all the same lies
we to believe about ourselves. We do not know if she was married or served alone.
We do know she was influential and trusted enough to carry Paul's letter to Rome.
This means she read them the letter and taught them what it meant! A powerful
woman in the early church, and she very well may have been single. This seems
countercultural to what we have been conditioned to believe.
In this season of singleness, how can you be an active and trusted member of your
church? Are you serving in a way that feels fulfilling? What would fulfilling service
look like, and how can you start getting there today? Ask God if the ideas you have for
your service are as big as His plans for you.

_____

_____

_____

_____

_____

_____

_____

_____

_____

_____

Day 4

I want you to take a few minutes to do a quick search about Deborah.

She was the only female Judge of Israel, a prophet, and present during a critical military movement for Israel. In the passage, the prophecy in Judges 4 is delivered and fulfilled by a woman. Throughout scripture, we see God use the voice of women in critical moments.

If you're not speaking up now, how are you going to speak up for and into your future family? How are you using your voice for the gospel? Are you speaking into others' lives in critical moments? Is your voice heard when you speak?

_____

_____

_____

_____

_____

_____

_____

_____

_____

_____

_____

_____

Day 5

Do you believe you have value within the body of Christ as a single woman? Paul is clear in his conviction that it's better to be single than to be married and have more time to dedicate to the Gospel.

Do you believe this? Do you see this value reflected in the way you serve? If you don't serve while single, when your time is accountable to no one, you won't serve when you have a family. Do you need to lean in more now to make it a value before you're in a relationship?

_____

_____

_____

_____

_____

_____

_____

_____

_____

_____

_____

_____

_____

Day 6

How does your church treat single people? Are you valued and given opportunities to serve to the fullest level despite your marital status? Are you proud of the way your church treats single people, or do you often leave feeling "othered" or less than? Pray through this reality, then ask God for your next steps. How can you either help make a change or continue to value all people at your church?

_____

_____

_____

_____

_____

_____

_____

_____

_____

_____

_____

_____

_____

_____

_____

Day 7

Day one of this week, you reflected on the Proverbs 31 woman. After spending a week learning more about women in the Bible and how you reflect them, I want you to go back to Proverbs 31 and re-study.

What felt new or different? Are you seeing her in a new light? Are you seeing yourself in a new light? Pray though your next steps.

_____
_____
_____
_____
_____
_____
_____
_____
_____
_____
_____
_____
_____
_____
_____

Week 9

Christ can't be the center of your relationship if He's not the center of your life. That may sound harsh, but it's true. If you want to have a Godly marriage, you need to live a Godly life. If you're not doing it now, when you are your primary or only responsibility and your time is accountable to no one but you, you're not going to when life is busier.

We have looked at Godly women who helped advance the Gospel in order to refute the lies that we are too much. This week we're going to look through the lens of what it means to live a Godly life.

We're not here for empty platitudes and encouragements. We're here to become Godly women, who live Godly lives, and build Godly communities. We're women who will have a spiritual legacy.

Our spiritual legacy doesn't start the day we have a kid or take a niece or nephew to church. It starts now with being faithful where God has us physically and relationally.

2 Timothy 2:2 gives the charge to take what we have learned about God, and impart it to others who will teach others. This is an action step to living a life that will create a spiritual legacy, the only legacy that is eternal. For you, it starts today!

Day 1

Proverbs 31 ends with this: "Charm is deceptive, and beauty does not last; but a woman who fears the Lord will be greatly praised. Reward her for all she has done. Let her deeds publicly declare her praise." Are you a woman who fears the Lord? The bigger question: do your actions publicly declare the Lord? Our actions, time, what we watch, read, and post are they adding to or detracting from spiritual legacy.
Pray about your spiritual legacy ask God for vision and strgenth to continue even when it's hard.

Day 2

Priscilla was a leader in the early church. She labored alongside Paul and eventually hosted the early church in Rome (Romans 16:5). She was a teacher (Acts 18:24), and Paul goes so far as to call her a co-worker in Christ (2 Timothy 4:19). She was a woman who dedicated her life to the Church, the gospel, and using her God-given gifts to expand the kingdom. If we could trace our Christian lineage back to the early church in Acts, I would be curious to see how many of us would be "descendants" of Priscilla. How many generations are on your spiritual family tree? Are you giving your life to the kingdom and advancement of the gospel? Who are your co-workers in Christ, and how can you use your God-given gifts for this holy work?

_____

_____

_____

_____

_____

_____

_____

_____

_____

_____

_____

Day 3

Have you heard of the daughters of Zelophehad? I hadn't until recently. They went to Moses requesting to inherit their father's land as he didn't have a son. They challenged and changed LAW in ancient Israel: daughters could inherit their father's land if he has no son. Talk about a legacy! A major breakthrough for the time, and today 40% of countries have restrictions on women owning land. These women were trailblazers while still being obedient to God. You can read about them in Numbers 36 and Joshua 17. Trailblazing for you can look completely different, but still make an impact for generations of women to come.

Pray and ask God what changes you can make that will change your legacy for your spiritual family, and the family you may create one day. How can you be obedient to Him while you do it?

_____

_____

_____

_____

_____

_____

_____

_____

_____

_____

Day 4

Last week we talked about Paul telling the Corinthians he believed it better to be single and more fully devoted to the gospel (1 Corinthians 7:32–35).
Personally, I have found so much purpose in dedicating my life to raising up the next generation of Christians. I know I have so much capacity because I don't have a husband or kids, and I get to use that energy to disciple, teach, and lead at my church. Pray about the following: What are you doing with your extra capacity? Where are you finding your purpose and using your gifts? What is your spiritual legacy?

_____

_____

_____

_____

_____

_____

_____

_____

_____

_____

_____

_____

_____

_____

Day 5

Ruth was obedient and faithful. She was teachable and willing to follow Naomi's advice. Most importantly, she was faithful to God. By following the Old Testament principles of redemption, Ruth became the great-grandmother of King David and part of the lineage of Jesus! Her spiritual legacy literally pointed to Christ.

But before any of that, Ruth had to be obedient and faithful to God while she was single. It's so easy to think, "I'll do ___ once God answers my prayers for a husband." Maybe your obedience in this season will position you where God needs you to meet your future husband, or fulfill His greater plan for your life.

Pray and be honest with yourself and with God. Where do you need to grow in faithfulness or obedience to Him right now? Where do you feel Him leading you and what's keeping you from going there?

_____

_____

_____

_____

_____

_____

_____

_____

_____

_____

Day 6

Depending on your spiritual background these two weeks may have involved unlearning a lot of bad theology and discovering what the Bible actually says about women and our role in the Great Commission. I hope now you can see yourself as valuable to God and fully equipped to make disciples.

Take some time to reread the narratives of these women and their roles. After pray about your role: what you need to change, what truths do you need to believe, or steps you need to take to have a greater legacy?

_____

_____

_____

_____

_____

_____

_____

_____

_____

_____

_____

_____

_____

_____

_____

_____

_____

Day 7

The past few weeks we studied women from the Bible who were leaders in their communities and had incredible legacies. Some married, some single.
Pray and ask God for clarity on your spiritual legacy. What do you think God has for you? Prayerfully write a vision statement about your life.

_____

_____

_____

_____

_____

_____

_____

_____

_____

_____

_____

_____

_____

_____

_____

_____

_____

_____

_____

Week 10

We were created for connection and community. We see it all through scripture, and we can even see it in our Creator. God is 3 in 1, Father, Spirit, and Son, always in perfect community with one another. We were created to reflect our Creator, and one of the ways we reflect Him is our need for community.

Before God created woman, He looked at Adam and said, "It is not good for man to be alone," so He made Eve to be his companion (Genesis 2:18). Hebrews 10 and Acts 2 talk about spurring each other on in faith, sharing meals, committing together to fellowship and ministry.

In community, we get to see the body of Christ come to life, and everyone uses their gifts to expand the kingdom. Our community is to rejoice with us and mourn with us. Community is there for the good and the bad; they're how we grow and how we remain in the faith.

We work our faith out together, in community. In a society that teaches radical individualism that leads to independence, the Bible shows us how we were created to depend on God and God's people. We were made to multiply our faith and do so in community.

This week we're talking about community. I believe life is way more fun and just better when we do it together. We're going to find our community, we're going to be real with them, and grow together as we pursue God above all else.

Grab your Bible, this week we'll be focused on reflecting on scripture.

Day 1

Read Hebrews 10:24–25 and Acts 2:42–47.

These verses tell us a few things. Community, at a basic level, involves shared faith, worship, and caring for one another. The loneliness you may feel won't be healed in a romantic relationship, but can be healed in community. The wounds we processed won't be healed in dating; they'll be healed in community. The calling you have on your life, the legacy you want to leave, isn't on hold until you're married, rather to be lived out in community.

Meditate on these passages and this truth. Ask God to bless you with community, or give you the courage to dive deeper into the community you have.

_____

_____

_____

_____

_____

_____

_____

_____

_____

_____

_____

_____

_____

_____

Day 2

Read 1 Corinthians 12:12–14. The body of Christ is how believers' gifts come together to reflect the whole of Christ. We all have different gifts; we all have a piece or the puzzle, none of us have the whole. It's beautiful to see community and coming together is part of how we as believers spread the gospel.

What gifts do you have? How does your community make you stronger? How do you come together to more fully reflect Christ? If you don't see your gifting, be real and ask your community to tell you what gifts they see in you.

_____

_____

_____

_____

_____

_____

_____

_____

_____

_____

_____

_____

_____

_____

_____

Day 3

Read Romans 12:10–13. Community thrives when love, respect, and generosity guide relationships. The idea of loving one another above ourselves is radically different. Devotion is defined as love, loyalty, and enthusiasm for a person or, in the case of community, people. Through Christ we are deeply devoted to our community, but we can only be as devoted as we are real. Your community cannot help you heal if they don't know what's broken.

Do you feel like you are devoted to your community, and do you feel like they are devoted to you? Are you real with them? What forces drive your relationships?

_____

_____

_____

_____

_____

_____

_____

_____

_____

_____

_____

_____

_____

_____

Day 4

ead Galatians 6:1–3. True community helps in a time of need and keeps us on track. Our community is made up of the people who ask us hard questions and tell us hard truths. It was through rich community that I could be asked if one season of waiting was preparing me for a harder season of waiting. It's in community that I can share the heartaches of wanting a husband and I can be challenged to grow to be ready when he does come along.

Pray about what you need to share with your community so they can challenge you to grow and help carry your burdens?

_____

_____

_____

_____

_____

_____

_____

_____

_____

_____

_____

_____

_____

_____

Day 5

Read 1 Thessalonians 5:9–28. This passage paints a beautiful picture of community, strengthening, encouraging, and praying for one another.
What about this community stands out to you? What do you have? What do you want more of? How are they helping you grow as you wait for Lord to answer your prayers?

_____

_____

_____

_____

_____

_____

_____

_____

_____

_____

_____

_____

_____

_____

_____

_____

_____

_____

_____

Day 6

Read Proverbs 27:17. This verse is often used in talking about friendship, and I fully believe that friendship leads to community. But for this, we're talking about all your people, not just one friend.

How are they sharpening you and making you more like Christ? How is that sharpening refining you to be a better disciple-maker and leave a better legacy?

_____

_____

_____

_____

_____

_____

_____

_____

_____

_____

_____

_____

_____

_____

_____

_____

Day 7

Read Ecclesiastes 4:9–12. This passage highlights the importance of community. Community is one of God's greatest blessings, and prayer is powerful. Let's bless our community through prayer.

List your community by name. Write how you see God at work in each of them and how they help you grow. Then, write a short prayer for each person.

If you're feeling bold, tell them how they've helped you grow, and ask how you can be praying for them.

_____

_____

_____

_____

_____

_____

_____

_____

_____

_____

_____

_____

_____

_____

Week 11

Marriage is not something we're promised. We have no guarantee what God has for us in life is to be married. To have a husband and family to spend our days with and share our lives. Paul actually says he believes it's better to remain single and have more time to dedicate to spreading the Gospel. On the flip side, we see marriage as really precious and the marriage covenant as an unbreakable bond between woman, man, and God.

The Church is referred to as the Bride of Christ, His most precious and valuable gift. The Bible gives a good amount of direction on marriage.

How do we reconcile these realities with our hopes? Where does the truth of the Bible intersect with our desires? If God gives the "desires of our hearts" and we're single, how is that passage true? Will you be okay and live a full life if you remain single?

This week we're going to pray through the reality of not being guaranteed marriage and the truth of God answering all our prayers. We'll confront having desires, maybe not getting what we're praying for, and sit in the uncomfortable truth that maybe God's best for us doesn't include a man.

I always tell my youth students that we're not afraid to have hard conversations, and we're going to get real about everything. I'm telling you the same. This book isn't platitudes and empty words meant to encourage you and soften the pain of waiting. It's meant to help you become a stronger woman of God and process your desires around marriage.

Doing that work demands confronting the reality that some Christians are going to live a life of singleness. That doesn't make you any less loved, valuable or capable of doing amazing things for the Kingdom of God.

This week may be hard, but I believe it's a hard we have to go through to see the other side.

Day 1

The truth is, we're not promised marriage; we are promised God. Isaiah 54:4-7 reminds us we are redeemed by God, and not marriage. So often we make marriage an idol and forget the one who saved us.

Take some time to confess the ways you have made marriage, or the idea of your future husband, your idol and lost track of God in the process.

_____
_____
_____
_____
_____
_____
_____
_____
_____
_____
_____
_____
_____
_____
_____
_____

Day 2

Singleness is not second best, and single people are not to be second-class citizens of heaven or members of churches. 1 Corinthians 7 talks about this multiple times as a gift providing more freedom to serve God.

Do you really see singleness this way? I don't always, but I have seen the gift in being faithful and serving God even when I want something different. Take this to God, tell Him all your feelings about being single.

_____

_____

_____

_____

_____

_____

_____

_____

_____

_____

_____

_____

_____

_____

Day 3

Have you ever been told, if you desire marriage, God will give it to you because He gives us the desires of our hearts? I have. Not only is it not helpful, it's not true. Read Psalm 37:3–6. We are told if we take delight in God, then He will give us the desires of our hearts. If your delight is in God, then the desires of your heart will be from Him and for His glory.

Where is your desire for marriage from? Where are you finding your delight?

_____

_____

_____

_____

_____

_____

_____

_____

_____

_____

_____

_____

_____

_____

Day 4

Read Romans 8:26–28. This passage is about prayer and God working things for those who love Him. God works things out in ways we never understand, but for Him to work them out, we have to take them to Him. He works things out for our good EVEN when we don't understand. God is using your singleness for your good, even if you don't understand why, and even if it's not a season but a reality for life. I know this hurts to hear; it hurts to write.

How would you feel if God working out all things for your good, answers your prayer for marriage with a no?

_____

_____

_____

_____

_____

_____

_____

_____

_____

_____

_____

_____

Day 5

Is marriage an idol you need to lay down at the foot of the cross? What does that mean to you, and how can you continue to pray for it without it becoming an idol? Take a few minutes to journal your honest thoughts and then turn them into a prayer, surrendering marriage and asking for desires that reflect your delight being in Him.

_____

_____

_____

_____

_____

_____

_____

_____

_____

_____

_____

_____

_____

_____

_____

_____

_____

_____

Day 6

We have talked a lot about friendship, community, and prayer. Here's where it all comes together. I want you to write out everything you feel about being in a season of waiting. I want you to write out how you would handle a "no," and how a "no" would impact your value. Then I want you to pray and share all of that with someone you trust.

Bring someone into your heartache. Letting them into the heartache means they will also be able to rejoice with you when you celebrate God moving, even if that movement is away from marriage and closer to Him. Or maybe they'll stand by your side at your wedding and celebrate how God is faithful to our prayers. Don't do this alone; do it in community.

_____

_____

_____

_____

_____

_____

_____

_____

_____

_____

_____

Day 7

Why do you desire marriage? Is it to build a family, or satisfy a sexual desire? Is it to have a partner in ministry, then in life, or because it seems comfortable? Be brutally honest with God about the root of your desire. Revisit your prayers from earlier this week. Come back, and keep writing until you feel like you have said everything.

If you're feeling bold, I invite you to pray this: "God, if marriage is your best for me, let me actively and faithfully wait until you bring him into my life. But if it is not your best plan for me, I ask you remove this desire. Amen."

_____

_____

_____

_____

_____

_____

_____

_____

_____

_____

_____

_____

Week 12

What now? You're in the last week of this journal, and I hope you can see how God has changed and grown you over the past 3 months.

Hopefully, some of your past pain points feel a little bit healed. Maybe you have vision or clarity on what you're looking for in a husband. Hopefully, you see the richness in all the relationships around you. But what now? Where do you go from here?

Like we talked about last week, we are not promised marriage, but I do believe God is kind and gives us desires for a reason. I'm not promising you that you'll finish this journal and meet your husband the next day. But what I hope is upon finishing this journal you're more healed and more ready to meet him if he did walk into your life in 8 days.

This week we're going to focus on what now, what's next, and how to carry this intentionality into the rest of our lives. On average, it takes 3 months to develop a habit. My hope for you is that intentional prayer and reflection are a habit you started here and will carry into the rest of your life!

What's next? I don't know, but I can't wait to find out!

Day 1

James 5:7–12 tells us to patiently enduring until God's return. Paul writes, "you must be patient, take courage…" When you're waiting for God to move and answer prayers, you must be patient and have courage. Keep waiting, keep praying, remain faithful. We don't understand the mystery of God's timing; it's a huge part of our faith. But if we're faithful, often we get to see how He moved when we thought He was being silent or still.

Read James 5:7–12. I want you to do 2 things: Write bold, short prayers about healing, love, dating: whatever has been a theme for you. Write each in 1–2 sentences so you can come back and pray it again and again.

Then go back to week 1 and reread that bold, short prayer and, if it's accurate, write it here, if not rewrite the prayer.

Then, in as many words as needed, tell God how you're feeling about waiting. Do you need endurance? Do you feel patient or need courage to keep praying?

_____

_____

_____

_____

_____

_____

_____

_____

Day 2

James 5:14–18 talks about the power of prayer. Take a moment to read it.
We're going to pray through a few categories: What are your hardships? What are you grateful for? Where do you need healing? What sin do you need to confess?
Then, once you pray that, I want to encourage you to be bold enough to share something you prayed about with a friend. Maybe it's as bold as confessing to them, or asking them to join you in praying for something more personal.

_____

_____

_____

_____

_____

_____

_____

_____

_____

_____

_____

_____

_____

_____

Day 3

Everything changes when we have vision. That's why every company, team, and church has a vision statement. In Matthew 28:19–20, we're given a vision for our life as believers: we are to make disciples. Married or single, male or female, young or old, this is the vision for our lives. How we live that out is more specific to each of us and our giftings.

Pray through a vision for your life. Ask God to reveal to you how you can live His vision. Write it for your life as it stands right now, single and following God. What is your vision for your life?

_____

_____

_____

_____

_____

_____

_____

_____

_____

_____

_____

_____

_____

_____

Day 4

Recently I have been thinking a lot about legacy. When we think about it, it's often attached to someone who did something incredible; made the most money, won the most games. Legacy is almost always associated with something grand but rarely tied to marital status.

What kind of legacy do you want to have? How do you want to be remembered and talked about when you're gone? Do you want to be known for accomplishments? What are they? For how you make people feel or how you love others? How do you? Make it practical, and pray big.

_____
_____
_____
_____
_____
_____
_____
_____
_____
_____
_____
_____

Day 5

We've written a few short prayers to come back to when it feels hard or pointless, or like God isn't moving. We also need verses that tell the truth about who we are to return to when we start to believe God isn't moving how or when we want.

Read the following passages, then reflect and pray on them:

Psalm 27:14, Lamentations 3:25–26, Isaiah 40:31, Ecclesiastes 3:11, Galatians 6:9.

_____
_____
_____
_____
_____
_____
_____
_____
_____
_____
_____
_____
_____
_____
_____
_____

Day 6

Read back through some prayers from different weeks. Have you seen God answer any of those prayers, heal you, or grow you? Whatever you have seen God do thus far, He can do again, and He can do even more. We have a really big and all-powerful God; there is literally nothing He can't do!

Ask Him to reveal to you ways He has been faithful to you in the past. Then pray in faith for how you want to see Him move again.

_____

_____

_____

_____

_____

_____

_____

_____

_____

_____

_____

_____

_____

Day 7

I hope these past three months have helped you grow. Being in consistent communication with God tends to have that effect. I hope it doesn't stop here. Take some time to reflect on all the ways you and your faith have grown over these months. Thank God for how He has moved.

Then ask Him to give you a desire to continue this rhythm, greater clarity for your vision, hope for relationships to come, and faith that He is moving even when you don't see how.

_____

_____

_____

_____

_____

_____

_____

_____

_____

_____

_____

_____

_____

_____